Bodiam Castle

East Sussex

THE NATIONAL TRUST

The Battle over Bodiam

In 1385 Sir Edward Dalyngrigge, a future royal councillor and veteran of the wars with France, received permission from the King to build a castle on his manor at Bodiam. The building that he raised, although now a ruin, is one of the most celebrated castles in England. It is visited every year by 170,000 people, and pictures of its walls and towers, peacefully reflected in the waters of the moat, appear on everything from book covers to jigsaw puzzles.

The popularity of Bodiam is not difficult to explain. Few buildings can rival its magnificent setting, and the embattled exterior of the castle itself is everyone's idea of what a medieval stronghold should look like. Bodiam has come to be considered as the last great English castle, before gunpowder and strong government made it irrelevant.

But the conventional appreciation of Bodiam Castle is now being challenged, and this icon of the Middle Ages has become quite as controversial as it is famous. Some scholars now argue that Bodiam was not a serious fortification at all, but a grand house designed with the architectural trappings of defence – such as battlements and arrow loops – solely to impress visitors and advertise the knightly class of its owner. If Bodiam is more a mock-stronghold than a real one, then we need to rethink our understanding not only of this building, but of the whole subject of castle architecture. Castles have always been thought of as essentially military buildings, whose architecture developed in response to technological changes in warfare. But if chivalric display and social advertisement also influenced their architecture – and the castle, therefore, had a peaceful aspect – then these buildings have been fundamentally misunderstood.

A consensus has still to emerge in this vigorous debate, but already, much to the surprise of both sides, Bodiam Castle has proved a much more remarkable and complex building than anybody had supposed. Its superb landscape setting turns out to have been deliberately conceived in the 14th century, and its architecture subtly contrived for grand effect. Bodiam was also part of a great flowering of late medieval secular architecture, whose sophistication has never been fully appreciated.

This debate is not just the preserve of scholars. Much of the evidence for the discussion is to be found in the fabric of the castle itself, and by looking at it carefully, you can form your own conclusions. Whatever you finally decide, however, you will leave in no doubt of the ingenuity with which this remarkable building was designed.

Castle ownership during the Middle Ages was a mark of lordly status. So Bishop Wyville of Salisbury (*d.*1375) chose to be depicted on his funerary brass framed within Sherborne Castle, Dorset. This is represented by a fantastical array of fortifications and with a champion at the gate. Some believe that Bodiam's defences were also purely decorative, intended to glorify its owner

Look at the various arrow and gun loops. Some are set in very restricted spaces and others have thick rimmed openings that must have made shooting at an angle difficult. Could you use them in war, or are they purely for show?

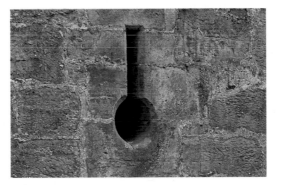

Bodiam Castle may appear formidable. But is it anything more than a piece of architectural theatre, admired in the Middle Ages for its splendour and setting? It is for you to decide

Sir Edward Dalyngrigge

Sir Robert Knollys, whose arms appear on the postern gate, is here shown leading a raid around St Omer and Noyon in July 1369. Knollys began his military career as an archer and rose to be a successful commander

Flanking Dalyngrigge's unicorn crest and coat of arms on the Gatehouse are the arms of his wife, Elizabeth Wardeux (*left*), and the Radynden family (*right*), previous owners of Bodiam

We know frustratingly little about Sir Edward Dalyngrigge, the builder of Bodiam. He was born into a minor Sussex gentry family which took its surname from Dalling Ridge near East Grinstead, where it had modest landholdings. Both his father and elder brother, Roger, who died childless in 1380, made advantageous marriages to wealthy heiresses. Dalyngrigge inherited their combined property, and added that of his wife, Elizabeth Wardeux. Through her in 1377 he acquired considerable landholdings both in and beyond the county, including the manor of Bodiam. In later life he probably enjoyed an annual income of £200–300, five or six times that required for the dignity of a knight.

As well as amassing an impressive inheritance, Dalyngrigge was active in pursuing his fortunes abroad. Throughout much of the 14th century, England was at war with France, and the members of many knightly and noble families fought in this conflict, the so-called Hundred Years War. Between 1359 and 1387 Dalyngrigge took part in a large number of military expeditions. Among the captains with whom he served were two Earls of Arundel, father and son, the premier figures of the Sussex nobility. He probably also had connections with Sir Robert Knollys, a veteran of the French wars, whose coat of arms appears above the Postern gate at Bodiam. Aside from these military expeditions, Dalyngrigge also served in Italy in 1367 and probably again in 1370.

Dalyngrigge's extensive landholdings and prolonged military service abroad made him a wealthy man with excellent court connections, and from the 1370s he began to play an active role in administering his native county. He helped to organise the defence of Sussex as a Commissioner of Array after 1377, and in 1380 was appointed a Justice of the Peace. During the following decade he was regularly returned as an MP, and in 1384 he even led local opposition to the King's uncle, John of Gaunt, who was tightening control over his Sussex estates. Dalyngrigge was successfully prosecuted by John of Gaunt on several counts, including trespass. He behaved with blustering defiance in court, twice throwing down his gauntlet in a challenge to personal combat.

By the time Dalyngrigge received a royal licence to fortify his manor house at Bodiam in 1385, he was an important figure in local politics. To own a castle was a statement of rank and power, and whether Bodiam was a fortification or a folly, all are agreed that it was built to reflect his new-found standing. Sir Edward continued as a prominent figure in royal service into the early 1390s. He died some time before August 1393.

Dalyngrigge (left) in combat

The sack of a city

Building Bodiam

This extraordinary 1380s facsimile of a medieval charter, complete with an enamel counterfeit seal, on a brass plaque at Cooling Castle in Kent is without surviving parallel. The English inscription begins: 'Knoweth that beth and shall be/ That I am made in help of the country'. The Bodiam licence repeats this idea of castle building being for the public good

Bodiam may have been built in part as a response to the Peasants' Revolt of 1381, which Dalyngrigge helped to subdue. This illustration from Froissart's *Chronicles* shows Richard II in London during the troubles

The construction of Bodiam probably got underway after Richard II granted a 'Licence to Crenellate' the building on 20 October 1385. By this licence, Dalyngrigge was given permission to 'strengthen with a wall of stone and lime, crenellate [add battlements] and make into a castle his manor house at Bodiam, next to the sea, for the defence of the adjacent country and resistance to the king's enemies'.

This licence is the main evidence that Bodiam Castle was built with a specifically military role in mind. Aside from the explicit statement that the castle was to secure the locality for the King, its particular terms seem to suit the political circumstances of the 1380s. During the previous decade the tables had turned in the Hundred Years War, and the French were raiding the English coast nearby.

Rye and Folkestone were burnt in 1377, and Winchelsea sacked in 1380. There was an invasion scare in the summer of 1385, when an invading army from across the Channel was constantly expected. There were also serious domestic problems. In 1381 crop failure and high wartime taxation sparked off the so-called Peasants' Revolt, which affected large areas of the country.

Those convinced that Bodiam is a sham fortification argue that the language of the licence to crenellate, which was framed by Dalyngrigge, is empty rhetoric. The defence of the realm, presented as the principal function of the new castle, was commonly invoked to justify constructing castles in this period, but Dalyngrigge may have seen it rather as a passport to respectability: castle ownership was a mark of noble rank. He is saying precisely what he ought to say while petitioning for the privilege to crenellate his residence. A modern analogy would be a politician on the eve of an election claiming that they want to reduce taxation. Of course, in both cases the speaker may really intend what they say, but they need to be judged by deeds, not words.

Contrary to the exact terms of the licence, Dalyngrigge did not castellate the existing manor house at Bodiam, which probably stood to the north where the farmhouse can be seen today. Instead, he set out his new residence on a fresh site, half-way up a hillside in the valley of the River Rother. He may have chosen this location so that the castle could command the river, a potential avenue for French attack. But the river was probably not a major route to Bodiam by 1385, and the closest threat was from the coast itself,

which was then about ten miles away. A more probable explanation is that the new site had natural springs. These still rise around the castle and were used to feed an extensive system of artificial pools, of which the moat is the sole survivor.

Who Dalyngrigge employed to design his new castle is not known, but it is commonly attributed to Henry Yevele, a royal mason. Yevele was involved in numerous building projects in Kent at this time, including work at Canterbury, Rochester and Cooling Castle. He acted as a consultant at Cooling, preparing the designs and only occasionally visiting the site. Whatever Yevele's role at Bodiam, the castle was not, as it is often represented, an isolated work of architectural genius. It is firmly rooted in an essentially English architectural tradition and is remarkable chiefly because it has survived. Most of the buildings to which it would have been compared are now lost or largely ruined.

Because battlements gave a building the status of a castle, they were a popular decorative device. At Bodiam, they appear properly on the walls and towers; half scale on the turrets; and in miniature around the rims of the castle chimneys and on the fireplace of Dalyngrigge's Great Chamber

Later History

Very little is known about the medieval history of Bodiam. Of the progress of construction and the completion of the castle after 1385, no evidence survives, nor are there any details about life here during the time of its builder. When Dalyngrigge died, the castle was inherited by his son, Sir John, and descended from him within the family until the male line died out in 1470. It then passed by marriage to the Lewknor family. One member of this family, a certain Sir Thomas, became implicated in agitations against Richard III in 1483. He apparently retired to the castle with a group of supporters, and a force was raised to besiege it. There is no record that a siege took place, however, and Sir Thomas probably surrendered without a fight.

After this episode, the castle and estate were briefly held by the Crown, before being passed back to the Lewknors and divided up between their descendants. In 1623 Sir Nicholas Tufton, later 1st Earl of

The tomb brass of a Dalyngrigge, probably Edward's brother, Sir Walter

Bodiam in 1777

8

Thanet, bought most of the property, including the castle. This was the first in a series of outright purchases that continued into the 20th century. Sir Nicholas's son, John, was a prominent Royalist during the Civil War and was compelled to sell the estate after Parliament imposed a massive fine in 1644. Most experts assume that the castle was deliberately ruined at this time, although there is no evidence that it was inhabited, or even used, at any point after the 15th century.

For most of the 18th century Bodiam was in the hands of the Webster family, and it is during their period of ownership that the castle began to be widely appreciated as a romantic ruin. The first view of Bodiam was engraved by Nathaniel Buck in 1737, and there are numerous depictions of it from the late 18th century onwards. These show that the ruins were overgrown with ivy, and that the castle courtyard was laid out with vegetable beds.

This is a replica of the bombard, probably of 15th-century date, which was dredged out of the moat in the 18th century. Although medieval guns look faintly ridiculous to modern eyes, the firepower of great siege trains in this period could devastate castles

The interior of Bodiam in 1782, by James Lambert. This view of the south side of the castle courtyard shows the ruins overgrown with vegetation. There is a cottage built into the back of the Postern Tower and the courtyard is laid out with vegetable beds

The Rescue

The remains of the two medieval wooden bridges to the castle were exposed in 1919, when Lord Curzon drained the moat. From the evidence of the timbers, both seem to have been deliberately dismantled while still in perfectly good repair

(*Right*) Lord Curzon, who restored the castle and bequeathed it to the National Trust

(*Opposite*) The ivy-covered barbican as it was before being restored by Lord Curzon. At this time the castle moat was still crossed by an earth embankment

In 1829 the castle was bought from the Webster family by John Fuller of Brightling, Sussex, for £3,000. This purchase marked a watershed in Bodiam's history. Allegedly, Fuller bought the property to save it from demolition, and from his time forward all its owners have been actively concerned to preserve and restore it. Fuller restored the Postern Tower and provided the present oak door to the castle gate. The next purchaser, however, undertook much more extensive repairs. George Cubitt, later created Lord Ashcombe, purchased the castle from Fuller's nephew in 1864 for about £5,000. He had the buildings surveyed

and thoroughly restored, replacing collapsed masonry and consolidating various parts of the ruin. In a concession to the contemporary taste for the romantic, however, he left the castle walls overgrown with plants and ivy.

The contribution of both Fuller and Cubitt has been rather overshadowed by that of the castle's last private owner, Lord Curzon. George Nathaniel Curzon is a figure of enormous importance in the history of architectural conservation in Britain and beyond. He first showed an interest in restoring monuments in India, where, as Viceroy, he helped to protect the Taj Mahal at Agra. When he returned to England, he turned his attention to monuments in this country, introducing the first Act for the Preservation of Ancient Monuments.

Lord Curzon was captivated by Bodiam when he first chanced upon it and in 1917 bought the castle, initially intending to make it habitable again. Nothing came of this plan, and instead, in 1919, he set in hand a less radical conservation project, supervised by William Weir, an architect much used by the Society for the Protection of Ancient Buildings. Curzon drained and excavated the moat, revealing the wooden footings for the original bridges to the castle and numerous small finds, including bits of armour and cannonballs. As well as restoring the building, Curzon wrote a lavishly produced book on the castle, which was published posthumously in 1926, the year Bodiam came to the National Trust under the terms of his will.

Tour of the Castle

The Setting

One of the most remarkable discoveries about Bodiam in recent years is that the castle was the centrepiece of an elaborately conceived landscape, much as great country houses were in later centuries. A survey in 1988 revealed the existence of six pools, besides the moat, terraced into the hill. Originally, these clustered around the moat and were presumably intended to set off the building to advantage. The original approach would have been from the north, and so it is still possible to imagine the drama of arriving here in the 14th century, with the castle reflected in sheets of water.

Throughout the Middle Ages water was widely used in the setting of buildings. The ambitious scale of some medieval water landscapes can still be appreciated at Framlingham and Kenilworth castles. Lakes and moats appear to have had a symbolic and aesthetic appeal. In the case of many manor houses, for example, the residential buildings alone are enclosed within the moat, as if the water physically and visually defined the heart of the house.

Water also had an obvious defensive value, but whether it did at Bodiam is hotly contested. The moat itself is retained against the slope of the hill for nearly half of its circumference by a dam of earth. Because this could easily be breached and the moat drained, some historians have argued that this feature was militarily useless.

Of the wider setting of the castle, little is now known. Mention is made in the 15th century of a park at Bodiam, but its extent is not clear. Hunting was a lordly sport, and so enclosed parkland, provided with good game, was often one element in the setting of an important residence. So too was farmland, which remained the principal source of wealth throughout the Middle Ages. Castles were presented as offering the security which made farming possible, and an approach to one through a fine estate, studded with barns and mills, reflected both prosperity and good lordship. A mill was built in 1386, which probably stood to the south-west of the castle, on the hill immediately below the moat with the flat enclosed area to the south-west of the castle enclosing the millpond. In 1383 Dalyngrigge also obtained a licence for a market and fair at Bodiam, as if he was already planning a model estate with a new castle at its heart.

Perhaps to admire the entirety of his creation, Dalyngrigge appears to have constructed the terrace which runs along the hedgeline at the top of the field behind the castle. On this have been discovered the foundations of a substantial medieval building, which may have been a gazebo, intended to offer fine vistas of the castle below, set against its surrounding pools.

Poitiers Castle, from the *Trés Riches Heures du Duc de Berry* of about 1415. This idealised image of a castle landscape shows peasants toiling amidst rich estates. An inner moat separates the heart of the castle from a cluster of service buildings outside

(*Right*) Old Scotney Castle in Kent and many other late 14th-century castles and manor houses were set in pools, although few have survived as well as Bodiam

(*Opposite*) Bodiam Castle was the centrepiece of a formal medieval landscape, of which the moat is the last element to survive. This view (from private land) is taken from a terrace on the hillside above the castle, which may have been used as a viewing platform in the 14th century. From here, one could admire the building in its ornamental setting

The Postern tower in the middle of the south front originally served as a back entrance with its own bridge (now gone)

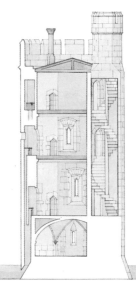

The Exterior

Viewed from the edge of the moat, the exterior of Bodiam still appears much as it must have done in the Middle Ages. The castle is designed on a regular, square plan. At each corner there stands a drum tower and, midway along each wall, one of rectangular plan. Two of the rectangular towers form gateways into the castle on opposite sides of its enclosure. The largest of these, which serves as the castle entrance today, faces north into the hillside. Overlooking the valley towards the south is a smaller gatehouse tower, popularly known as the Postern. It was formerly approached over a wooden bridge that ran straight across the moat in front.

The overall effect of the castle exterior is so immediately satisfying that few people notice what ingenious visual tricks the architecture plays. Viewed from within, Bodiam is a small building, but from outside it appears impressively large. One reason for this is that the moat distances the observer and isolates the castle from objects that might give it scale. This makes the blank exterior walls, set with small windows, look much larger than they really are. The staircase turrets attached to each tower were also kept as small as possible in order to make the towers look big by comparison.

This play with proportions is only one of the mannerisms of the exterior. For a building of this date, its windows are very oddly designed. Those in the towers are neither arrow loops nor proper windows. Their form could reflect an architectural compromise between comfort and defence. But if so, it seems odd that there should

also be two large windows for the Chapel and the Hall. Like the tower openings, these are ruggedly detailed, in marked contrast to the decorated window patterns of the castle interior. There can be no defensive explanation for this absence of ornament, and it suggests a deliberate attempt to make the exterior look forbidding.

Even in their ruined state, the clustering of towers and stair turrets, crowned with battlements, still give the building a slightly fantastical air. Numerous tall chimney-stacks would have added to the effect of this busy outline. A few still survive and are topped with miniature battlements – a delightful echo of the full-scale architecture. When Curzon drained the moat, he also discovered the collapsed remains of a low crenellated wall around the outer face of one side of the moat. Like the chimney detailing, this must have been a purely decorative feature. Dalyngrigge was evidently determined that no visitor could doubt his right to castellate Bodiam.

(*Left*) A cross-section of the south-east tower. Bodiam's corner towers are remarkably compressed, incorporating four storeys and a parapet in a structure only 20 metres high. Each floor forms a self-contained bedchamber, with its own fireplace and latrine, which emptied via a chute into the moat

(*Opposite*) Bodiam from the north-east. Medieval architects often liked to make the position of important rooms apparent on the outside of their buildings. The chapel is clearly indicated both by its large Gothic window and its outline, which projects beyond the regular plan of the castle

The Bridge and Barbican

The medieval bridge to the Postern tower has never been rebuilt, so today you enter the castle by its main gate, crossing the moat in a straight line from the north bank. Originally, a bridge ran from the western (right) bank of the moat, where a stone footing is still discernible, to the octagonal island at its centre. This island, which is incorporated in the present entrance

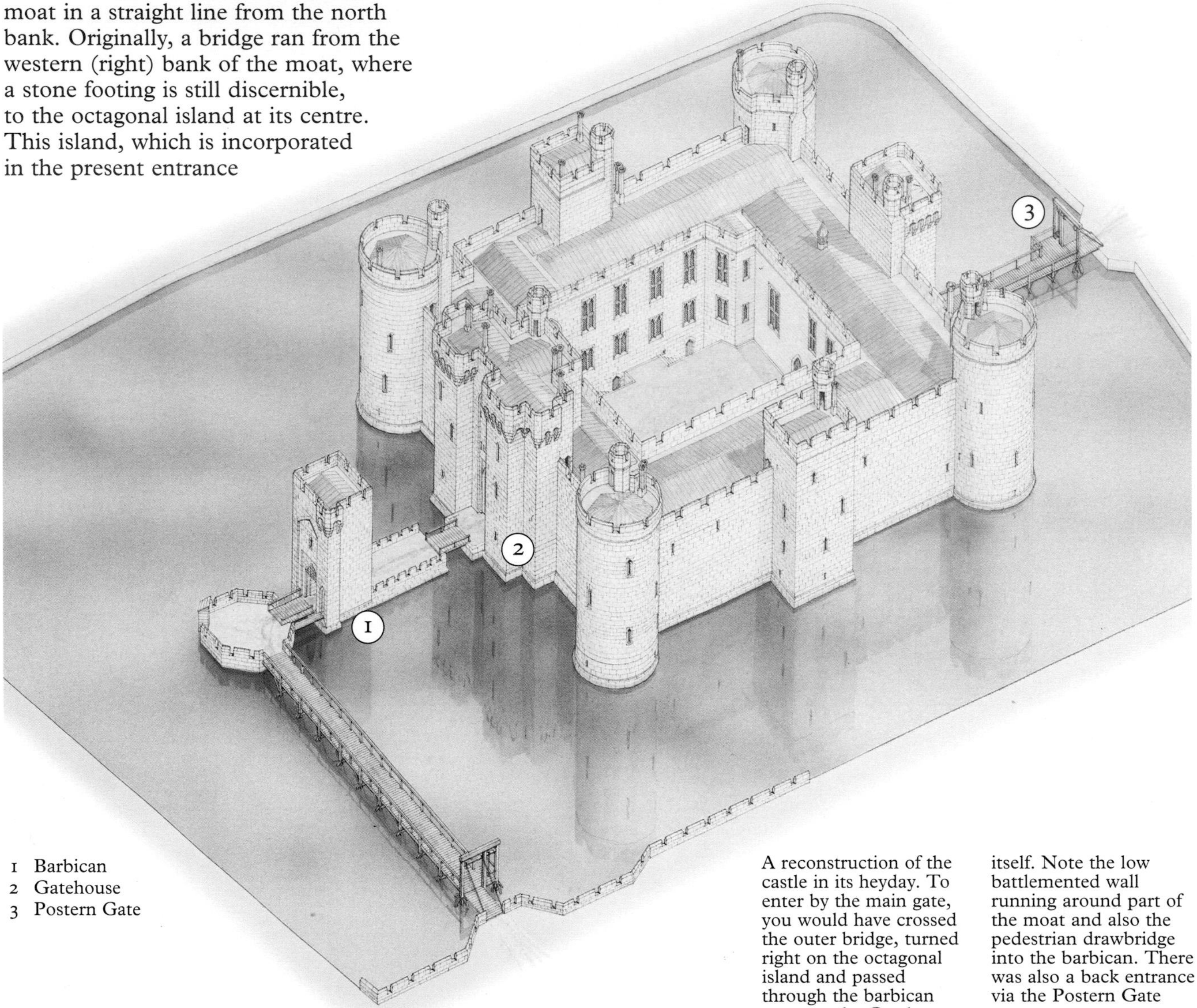

1 Barbican
2 Gatehouse
3 Postern Gate

A reconstruction of the castle in its heyday. To enter by the main gate, you would have crossed the outer bridge, turned right on the octagonal island and passed through the barbican tower to the Gatehouse itself. Note the low battlemented wall running around part of the moat and also the pedestrian drawbridge into the barbican. There was also a back entrance via the Postern Gate

arrangement, was probably enclosed by a low crenellated wall. You then turned right (south) on to the modern line of approach and crossed a short bridge (possibly a drawbridge) to a free-standing gate tower. Only a stump of masonry now survives from this outer defence, or barbican gate. Beyond the barbican there must have been another wooden bridge extending to the Gatehouse itself.

The original 'dog-leg' approach has traditionally been seen as a defensive device, ensuring that attackers had to pass directly under the walls of the castle in order to get to the main gate. But perhaps the whole design was really a piece of theatre to impress visitors. Various weaknesses in the defences of the Gatehouse suggest this.

The present-day approach to the Gatehouse

The Gatehouse

The Gatehouse is a magnificent building with two projecting towers, each crowned by a projecting fighting platform known as a machicolis. Set between the towers is the castle gateway, which is framed in a recess for a drawbridge and still has what may be its original iron-shod portcullis. In the faces of the surrounding Gatehouse walls are tiers of slit openings, some of which take the shape of an inverted keyhole. This is a characteristic design for a gun loop: the slit allowed the gunner to see his target, while the gun was run through the round hole at the base. Within the Gatehouse itself is a long passage defended by two further portcullises and covered by two vaults, one of which has now collapsed. Where the ribs of the vaults intersect there are ring-like openings, popularly known as 'murder holes', openings through which the defenders of the castle could drop objects on attackers.

But would these defences have worked? The arrow loops are too narrow and awkwardly placed for use, while the gun openings have such thick mouths that it would be possible only to fire straight out of them — a dangerous exercise in the case of the pair facing into the gateway. The murder holes are too small for effective use, and no drawbridge could have been fitted to the gatehouse, because the portcullis would have obstructed its mechanism. Finally, why would an attacker be so obliging as to assault this gate, when the Postern is so comparatively defenceless? After all, a castle is only as strong as its weakest point.

The openings in the vault over the main entrance have been described as 'murder holes', through which objects could be dropped on an attacker, but it is an open question whether they would ever have been usable, and in many cases they were purely decorative. Indeed, those in the Bloody Tower in London (1360–2) are filled with stone leopard's heads (*below*)

The Interior

Whatever the value of its defences, what remains of the interior of Bodiam shows that its lodgings were comfortable and well appointed. The castle buildings were constructed against the outer walls so as to create a handsome central courtyard enclosed by four regularly proportioned, two-storey ranges. Little survives of the walls facing on to the courtyard, but there are sufficient remains to give a good indication of what they originally looked like.

In most essentials, the buildings around the courtyard are arranged according to the classic medieval domestic plan. The Great Hall and kitchen were situated in the range of buildings opposite the main gateway of the castle. Their principal entrance is aligned with the gate passage across the courtyard – a common nicety of design. Filling the range to the left (east) of the Gatehouse, and connected to one end of the hall, were the family's apartments. These included Dalyngrigge's Great Chamber and the castle chapel. The Gatehouse (north) range probably included space for storage and accommodation, but the range to the right (west) is more difficult to understand.

The two massive chimneys in the cross-walls at the centre of the west range have led some to suggest that it was a self-contained lodging for retainers, arranged with its own kitchen. But in their present form, the fireplaces are certainly not 14th-century, and a kitchen was probably

A reconstruction of the castle courtyard as it would probably have appeared to a medieval visitor entering from the main gate. The surviving walls are shown in a darker colour. The large door opposite leads

into the Great Hall range. Dalyngrigge's private apartments were in the range on the left. The grander rooms were on the first floor, which was lit by two-tier windows

established here only later. One detail suggests that the area once incorporated a staircase, entered from the courtyard door at ground level. Both doors on the upper floor in the fireplace walls face inwards. Such an arrangement is very curious and would be best explained if there was a landing at this point giving access into the first-floor rooms to either side. The rooms themselves had large windows facing on to the courtyard and might have been secondary formal chambers.

Such is the coherence of the inner courtyard design that it is usually described as having been planned when the castle was first laid out. The truth is probably slightly more complicated. If you walk towards the chapel on your left and turn to face the south-east corner of the Gatehouse, you can see evidence of an important medieval alteration. The mouth of the present gate passage projects like a porch into the courtyard behind the Gatehouse. Although built in the same style as the main body of the Gatehouse, and therefore presumably of the same date, this porch-like structure must have been an afterthought. Not only does it obscure features of the Gatehouse, such as a stair window, but there is a clear division between the stonework in the two parts of the building. This alteration is important, because the line of the inner courtyard wall is determined by the length of the present gate passage. Since this is the product of a change of plan, then the design of the courtyard may have been revised during its construction.

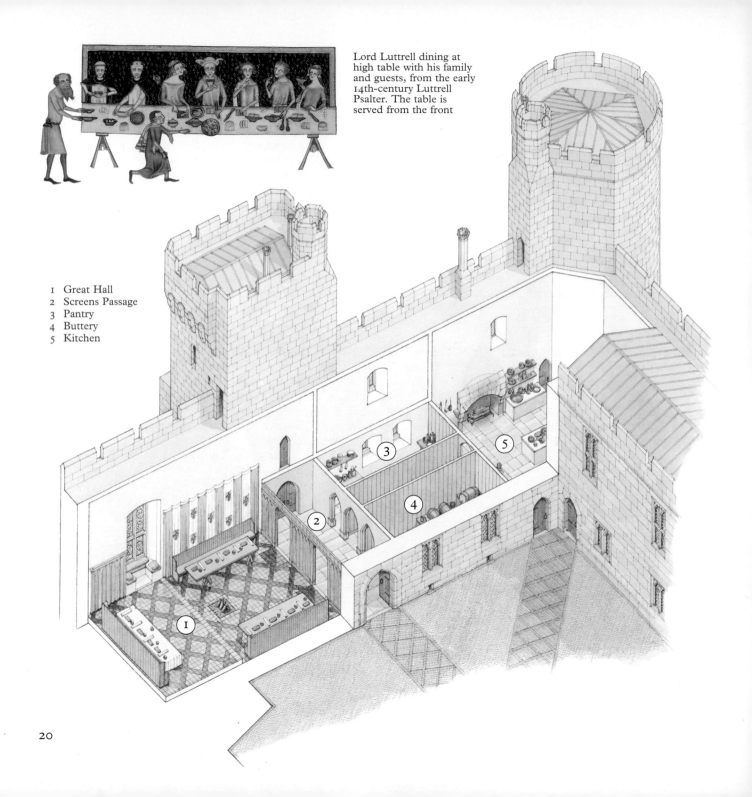

Lord Luttrell dining at high table with his family and guests, from the early 14th-century Luttrell Psalter. The table is served from the front

1 Great Hall
2 Screens Passage
3 Pantry
4 Buttery
5 Kitchen

The Public Castle

The Great Hall range was the domestic hub of the castle and is best understood when viewed from the courtyard. As is typical in medieval houses, this range is divided into two sections, the Great Hall to the left (east) and a series of service rooms, including a kitchen, to the right (west). It probably had a continuous, low-pitch roof, which was largely masked from the courtyard by a battlemented parapet. At the extreme left of the inner wall to the building was a stair turret leading up to Dalyngrigge's inner apartments, but only the foundations of this survive.

The Great Hall

As was typical in the Middle Ages, the Great Hall would appear to have been arranged with an open hearth in the centre and a dais at its so-called 'high' (eastern) end. Erected on the dais was a high table, at which Dalyngrigge would have dined on formal and public occasions. More usually, he would have eaten within his own

(Opposite) The Great Hall range followed the classic medieval plan. To the left is the Great Hall with its high table set on a dais at one end. The hall is shown furnished with striped hangings and a tiled floor, both characteristics of rich interiors in this period. There are tables set along the sides of the hall for the household, and the room is heated by a central hearth. Running across the middle of the range between its two principal entrances – the Postern gate and courtyard door – is the stone-flagged screens passage. Opening off this passage to the right through the cluster of three doors are the service rooms – the kitchen, buttery and pantry – with bare and functional interiors

apartments. Facing one another across the hall at its opposite, 'low', end were the principal entrances to the range, one through the Postern gate and one through the central courtyard doorway. These entrance doors would originally have been concealed from the body of the hall by a wooden screen running across the building.

The Kitchen

This screen would also have concealed the three arched doorways which presently stand isolated in the shell of the building – the service doors to the Great Hall. Those to either side led to two lost ground-floor chambers, the buttery and pantry. Above these rooms, at first-floor level, was a grand inner chamber. The central doorway led down a short passage to the kitchen. This rises the full height of the range and preserves two massive medieval fireplaces, as well as an oven chamber.

The South-West Tower

In the basement of the tower at this corner of the castle is a vaulted chamber with what is now a well. Since the water in it comes from the moat, and all the latrines emptied into this, there must be some doubt as to whether it could ever have served as a fresh water source. Another possibility is that it was originally a water tank, lined in lead, and filled by hand from another water supply. If you look up into the top of this tower, you can see a honeycomb of holes running round the walls of the upper floor. This is a dovecote, and the birds kept here provided food.

The three doorways in the screens passage led to the kitchen, pantry and buttery

The well in the south-west tower

The chapel window

The private chapel of Philip the Bold, Duke of Burgundy, pictured in a 14th-century manuscript illumination. The duke has no permanent closet, as exists at Bodiam, but kneels behind a curtain in a side-aisle, which served the same purpose

The Lord's Apartments

Arranged along the eastern side of the castle courtyard were the most important chambers in the castle, Dalyngrigge's inner apartments. Again, the original arrangement of this set of rooms is best appreciated from the courtyard. With a careful eye it is still possible to visualise this once-splendid series of interiors and understand how they would have unfolded to a medieval visitor. (For the sake of clarity, you should disregard the basement, the ceiling of which is quite clearly defined by a stone shelf running along the face of the outer wall beneath the ground-floor fireplaces.)

You entered the east range through a lobby and stair turret (2) set in the corner of the courtyard adjoining the upper end of the Great Hall. The site of this structure is marked by an irregular grass platform projecting into the corner of the courtyard. From this you could pass either straight into the ground floor of the east range or up to its first floor. Both levels were divided up internally to create two parallel sequences of chambers, one above the other. To judge from the numbers of windows and the enrichment of the central fireplace, the upper floor was the more important of the two suites.

There were three principal chambers on each floor. The two rooms at the far end of the range to your right (south) were probably antechambers to the apartments beyond. Beside the antechamber was the principal room on each floor, served by a large central fireplace, beyond which was an inner apartment that communicated with the Chapel. At ground-floor level it did so through a door, but upstairs there was a window into it both from the main chamber and from another small room opening beyond it. The latter was certainly a closet, a room from which it was possible to pray in private and watch Divine Service.

The arrangements on the upper floor of the east range clearly identify them as Dalyngrigge's own set of apartments. These could be described as an Outer Chamber (the antechamber), a Great Chamber (a dining and reception room), and an Inner Chamber (where Dalyngrigge would have slept) with its attached closet and two subsidiary tower chambers. The floor below may have formed a parallel suite of chambers for Dalyngrigge's wife, Elizabeth, but it could equally have incorporated other formal rooms, such as a great parlour. Whatever function they served, they would have been well furnished. Dalyngrigge was not quite of the standing to possess fine tapestries, but coloured or painted hangings would have created a rich and comfortable interior.

A cut-away reconstruction of the inner apartments in the east range, furnished in the style of the 1380s. The rooms are decorated with varying richness to reflect their importance, and the floors are laid with tiles or woven rush matting. Dalyngrigge's coat of arms is repeatedly displayed on glass, paint and fabrics. The principal apartments are on the upper floor, which was connected by a stair turret to the dais of the hall. From the panelled ante-room at the far end to the range the visitor entered the Great Chamber, richly decorated with painted hangings. Beyond is Dalyngrigge's bedchamber, comfortably hung in red worsted. There were two further inner chambers beyond the bedroom in the square tower. Overlooking the chapel (to the left) are two internal windows. One opens from the bedchamber itself and the other from Dalyngrigge's closet

1 Great Hall
2 Stair turret
3 Great Chamber
4 Dalyngrigge's bedchamber
5 Chapel

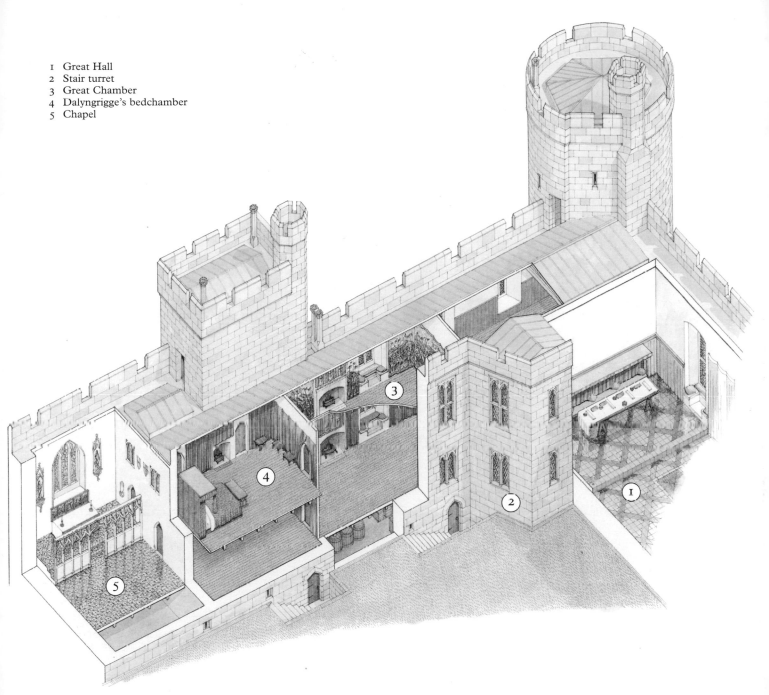

The Pill-box

On the way back to the car-park, it is worth turning aside to look at the brick pill-box, a relic of 20th-century war built under the shadow of this celebrated medieval castle. After the fall of France in May 1940, Britain was suddenly and unexpectedly faced with the threat of a German invasion. From what was known of German tactics, it was expected that intense air attacks would precede the assault, which would involve columns of tanks, accompanied by infantry divisions, punching rapidly inland from beachheads on the south-east coast. German paratroopers were also expected to play an important role behind the front line of enemy advance.

General Sir Edmund Ironside, Commander-in-Chief of the Home Forces, decided upon a policy of layered defence. Coastal fortifications were designed to break up and funnel attacks inland, so that the limited reserves of troops could be effectively used to counter any breakthrough. Inland, he created several lines of defence to slow down the German advance, using natural features, where possible.

The Bodiam pill-box was part of a defensive line along the River Rother, a natural tank barrier. It is built of brick and commands the bridge over the river 300 metres to the west. The pill-box comprises two chambers, the principal one for a six-pounder Hotchkiss anti-tank gun, and an annexe for machine-guns. Usually, pill-boxes were also surrounded by other defences, including trenches and machine-gun posts, although there are no traces of these at Bodiam today. The particular shape of the pill-box, with its angled annexe, is an unusual variation on the standard forms. It was manned by ten men from the Canadian Army and by the Home Guard, probably until 1944, when the threat of invasion had disappeared.

The pill-box and the castle: fortifications across six centuries